Map of Memory Lane

Story by Francesca Lynn Arnoldy

Art by YoungJu Kim

ISBN: 9781732780613

FIRST EDITION

www.FrancescaLynnArnoldy.com

To Gram, who fielded my unfiltered question about mortality thirty plus years ago with grace and a smile. — FLA

"Will you live forever?" Lee asked,
tracing a fingertip over the lines on Nana's familiar face.

"No, Lee, I will not," Nana replied with a gentle smile.

"I'll always be in your heart, though."

"How will I see you, Nana?"

"You'll see me on Memory Lane."

Lee rubbed a smooth stone and thought

for a moment, then asked,

"How will I get there?"

"First, you'll find a quiet spot," Nana began.

"Can it be inside?" asked Lee.

"Yes, it can."

"Can it be outside?" asked Lee.

"It sure can."

"Next, you'll close your eyes," Nana continued.

"In your mind, you'll picture a road. Along it,

there will be many places to explore."

"Like a map, Nana?"

"Yes, Lee, just like a map.

Each place along the map will be

a memory of a special time we spent together."

"Like the time we ate dessert for dinner?"

"Yes, that was so much fun!" Nana recalled.

"We baked gooey brownies and made fresh whipped cream."

"With raspberries on top!" added Lee, smiling.

"How about the time we splashed in the puddles
while it rained?"
"That was an adventure, wasn't it?" answered Nana.
"It finally stopped pouring, and then
we saw that double rainbow across the field."

"And what about all the stories you make up
about me while we color,

like *Lee the Willow Tree*, *Lee the Sweet Pea*,
and *Lee the Bumblebee?*"

"All of these memories—and more—will be on your map, Lee. Memory Lane is an amazing place where anyone can go when they want to remember someone."

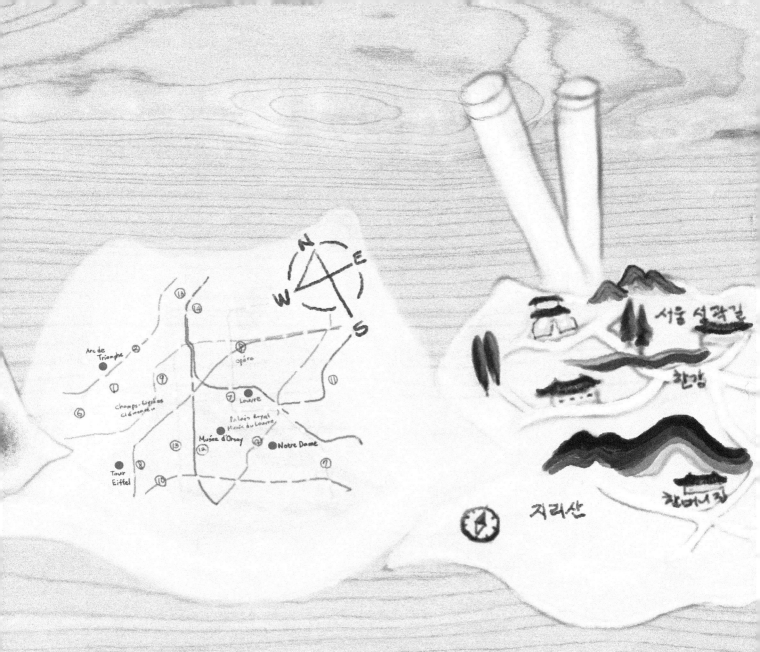

"Each person's map is unique...

depending on where they've lived,

who they've known,

and what memories they've created."

"Sometimes I take a trip down Memory Lane
when I'm missing someone," explained Nana.

"It doesn't take away all the sadness, but remembering makes me smile. Then, my heart aches a little less."

"So, I'll have my very own Memory Lane, Nana?"

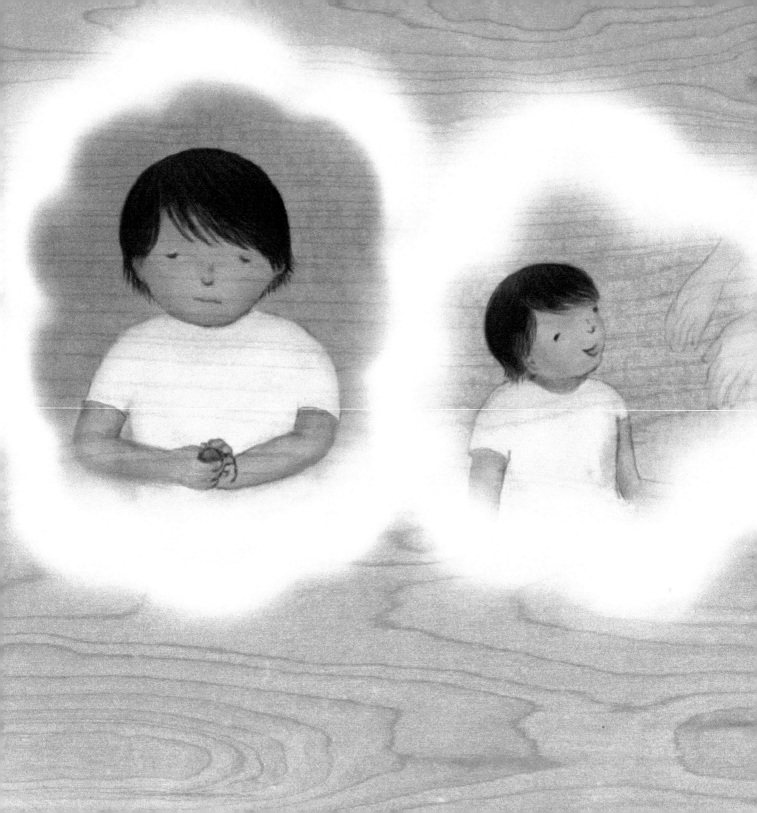

"Yes, Lee, you will. You'll be able to travel there whenever you like, if you're feeling sad or thankful or both."

Nana put her arm around Lee and said,
"Just like how a good hug can hold all sorts of feelings
and so much love, so can Memory Lane."

CPSIA information can be obtained
at www.ICGtesting.com
Printed in the USA
LVHW070313280122
709582LV00009B/345